To Mark - C.F.
To Zack and Luke - K.U.

OXFORD
UNIVERSITY PRESS

Great Clarendon Street, Oxford OX2 6DP

Oxford University Press is a department of the University of Oxford.
It furthers the University's objective of excellence in research, scholarship,
and education by publishing worldwide in

Oxford New York

Athens Auckland Bangkok Bogotá Buenos Aires
Cape Town Chennai Dar es Salaam Delhi Florence Hong Kong Istanbul
Karachi Kolkata Kuala Lumpur Madrid Melbourne Mexico City Mumbai
Nairobi Paris São Paulo Singapore Taipei Tokyo Toronto Warsaw

with associated companies in Berlin Ibadan

Oxford is a registered trade mark of Oxford University Press

Text copyright © Kaye Umansky 2001
Illustrations copyright © Chris Fisher 2001

The moral rights of the author and illustrator have been asserted

First published 2001

British Library Cataloguing in Publication Data available

ISBN 0-19-910752-1 (hardback)
ISBN 0-19-910753-X (paperback)

1 3 5 7 9 10 8 6 4 2

Printed and bound in Spain by Edelvives

Nonsense Animal Rhymes

Poems by *Kaye Umansky*

Illustrated by Chris Fisher

OXFORD
UNIVERSITY PRESS

Goldfish

Goldfish are **slippery**,
Goldfish are *wriggly*
Some are quite serious,
Some are quite *giggly*,
Some swim in circles
And wave when they pass,
Others make faces
And glare through the glass.
Wriggly, *giggly*,
Most of all, wet,
You can't beat a goldfish
If you want a pet.

Milkshakes

By day, the peaceful cows chew cud
And flick their tails in leafy shade.
At night, they turn cartwheels in mud
And that is how milkshakes are made.
My grandad says that this is true.
I think he's telling fibs, don't you?

Piggy Got Stuck Up The Chimney

Piggy got stuck up the chimney,
Piggy was much too stout,
We tied a sheet to his dangling feet,
POP! We pulled him out.

We washed him in the sunshine,
We dried him in the rain,
Then piggy got stuck up the chimney
And we had to start again.

Chess

I play chess with my cheetah.

My cheetah's name is Jim.

He has been known to beat me.

But, mostly, I beat him.

Yesterday I was defeated.

That's because my cheetah cheated.

Tortoise

I am a little tortoise,
My house is on my back.
I often stop and pop inside
To have a little snack.

And then I pop back out again
And smell the lovely flowers.
That is my daily exercise.
It takes me hours and hours.

My house is warm and cosy
And clean as a new pin.
And when my friends come calling,
I'm always out or in.

Little Birdie

Little birdie on the branch,
Very small and shy.
Tell me, birdie, can you talk?
No, kid. Can you fly?

Gorilla!

I'm a Gorilla!
I'm a Gorilla!
I want ice cream
And I want vanilla!
Three big scoops
On a dish, with a spoon.
I want ice cream
And I want it **SOON**.

Pussy Cat, Pussy Cat

Pussy cat, pussy cat,
Where have you been?
I've been sewing up socks
On the sewing machine.

Pussy cat, pussy cat,
Where are you going?
I'm off to a disco.
I'm fed up with sewing.

Lucky Ducky

Lucky Ducky
Played in muck,
Lucky Ducky
Got quite stuck.
He made the bank
Before he sank,
Plucky
 Mucky

   Yucky

    Lucky

     Ducky.

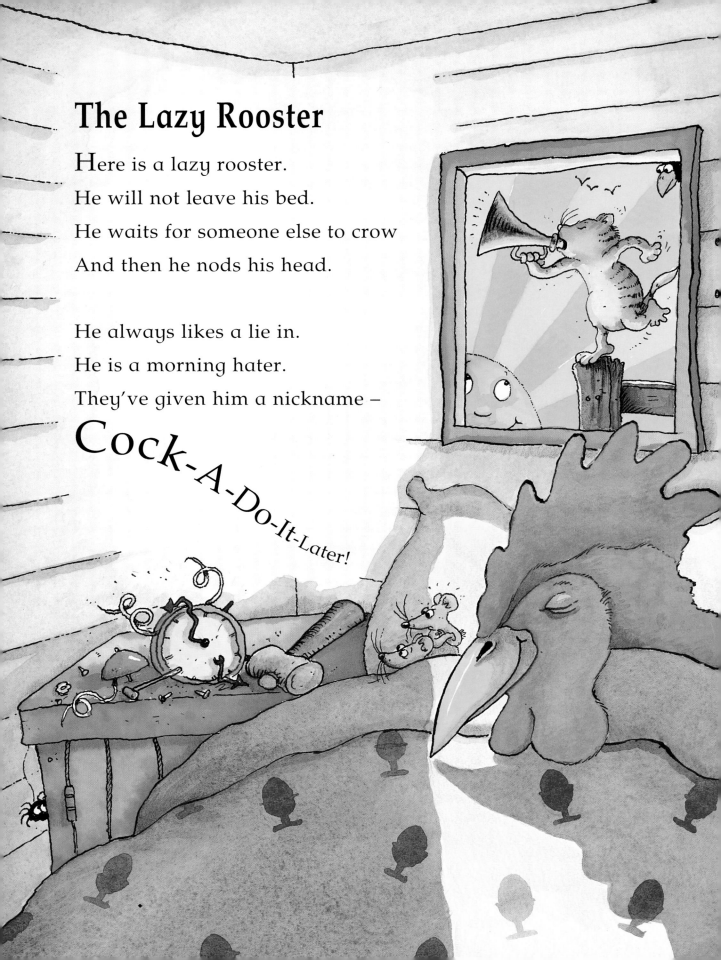

The Lazy Rooster

Here is a lazy rooster.

He will not leave his bed.

He waits for someone else to crow

And then he nods his head.

He always likes a lie in.

He is a morning hater.

They've given him a nickname –

Cock-A-Do-It-Later!

Tiger Joe

A worried young tiger called Joe
Had spots from his head to his toe.
He shouted, "Oh, cripes!
I'm supposed to have stripes!
I think I'm a leopard, you know!"

Mad Weather We're Having

It's raining cats and dogs again,
It said so on the news.
Last Sunday it rained penguins.
On Monday, kangaroos.

On Tuesday, it was froggy,
On Wednesday, cold as mice,
On Thursday, it snowed polar bears
(Which wasn't very nice.)

Friday was a fowl day,
Saturday was bats,
And now we're back to Sunday
With a load more dogs and cats.

I'd like to stay here talking
But I'm soaked right to the skin.
Now it's blowing up a buffalo!
I think I'm going in.

Elephants

Elephants are bashful,
As bashful as can be.
They always keep their trunks on
When swimming in the sea.

How unlike the polar bears,
Who do not seem to mind
And swim in freezing waters
With a polar bare behind.

Bad Hare

Harry Hare was late for school,

He dawdled in the lane.

He broke his brand new pencil

And his sums were wrong again.

He got sent off at football

And his homework blew away.

The teacher wrote his mum a note.

It was a Bad Hare Day.

St Jungles

The school is St Jungles,

And here are the staff.

Mr Gorilla

And Mrs Giraffe.

Old Mr Elephant,

Miss Chimpanzee

And Mr McMonkey

Who teaches P.E.

Ms Tiger cooks dinner,

She's one of the mums.

And Mr Puff-Adder,

He teaches us sums.

Bored

Brian the lion,
Samantha the panther
And Rita the cheetah
Were horribly bored.
So they stood on a hill
In deepest Brazil
And they **roared** and they **roared**
And they **roared** and they *ROARED!*

"Enough of this roaring,"
Said Brian the lion,
"My throat's really sore
And it's hurting my head.
I want to be quiet.
I think we should try it."
And so they went home
And played Twister™ instead.

The Wolf's Tale

I'm a Big, Bad Wolf.

My name is Keith.

I'll tell you my adventures.

I huffed and I puffed 'til I blew out my teeth

And had to get new dentures.

So now I cannot huff and puff

And am no longer snappy.

I moved in with the Little Pigs.

We're really, really happy.

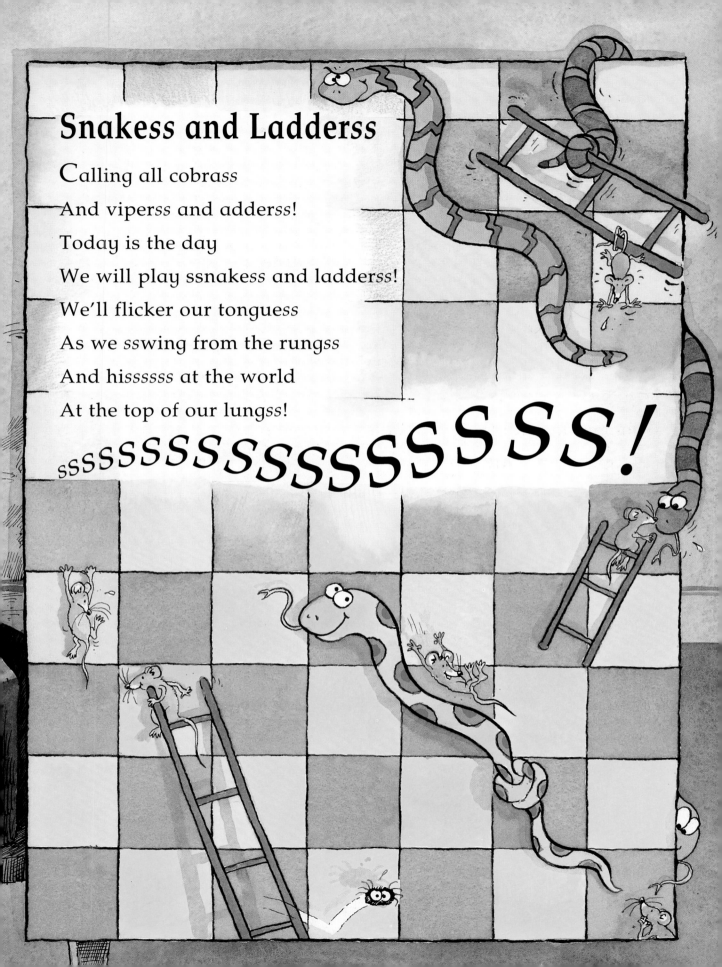

Snakess and Ladderss

Calling all cobrass
And viperss and adderss!
Today is the day
We will play ssnakess and ladderss!
We'll flicker our tonguess
As we sswing from the rungss
And hissssss at the world
At the top of our lungss!

sssssssssssssssSSSSSSSSS!

Poor Noah!

It's raining, it's pouring,
The lions are roaring,
The hippos are kicking
Great holes in the flooring!

The monkeys are shrieking,
The tigers aren't speaking
And both the giraffes
Are complaining of leaking.

The rabbits are jumpy,
The bears are quite grumpy,
And both of the camels
Have gone really humpy.

No wonder poor Noah
Was heard to remark
"It's hard keeping order
Inside of this ark!"

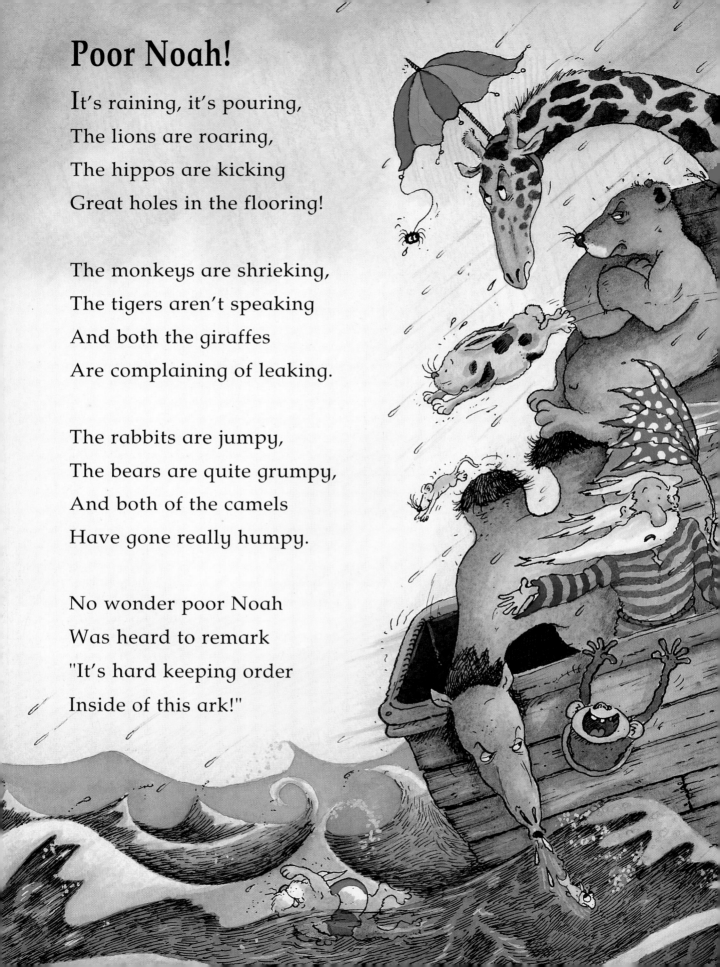

The Insect Race

Ready, steady, off they go!
The beetle's in the lead!
The grasshoppers are gaining,
With a sudden burst of speed.

The worm has turned the corner,
And the crowd begins to clap,
But the spider and the ladybird
Are closing up the gap!

They're heading for the winning post,
The pace is really fast.
The race is done. The beetle won.
And all the snails came last.

Rockaby, Crocodile

Rockaby, crocodile,
Deep in the ooze,
The moon's in the sky
And it's time for a snooze.
Tomorrow, we'll fish
In the rivers and streams.
But now it's your bedtime.
Goodnight, and sweet dreams.

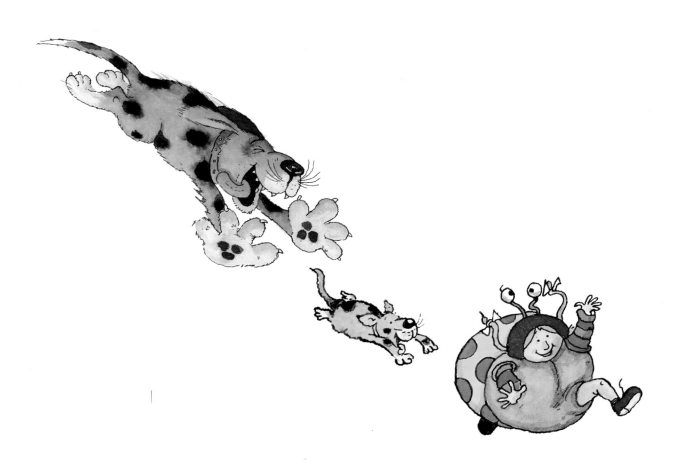